# PHOTO
# Tricks

## 100 Spot-the-Difference Challenges

Photographs by Robin Fox

## STERLING INNOVATION

An imprint of Sterling Publishing Co., Inc.

New York / London
www.sterlingpublishing.com

STERLING, the distinctive Sterling logo, STERLING INNOVATION, and the Sterling Innovation logo
are registered trademarks of Sterling Publishing Co., Inc.

2 4 6 8 10 9 7 5 3 1

Published by Sterling Publishing Co., Inc.
387 Park Avenue South, New York, NY 10016

Distributed in Canada by Sterling Publishing
c/o Canadian Manda Group, 165 Dufferin Street
Toronto, Ontario, Canada M6K 3H6
Distributed in the United Kingdom by GMC Distribution Services
Castle Place, 166 High Street, Lewes, East Sussex, England BN7 1XU
Distributed in Australia by Capricorn Link (Australia) Pty. Ltd.
P.O. Box 704, Windsor, NSW 2756, Australia

Sterling ISBN 978-1-4027-5970-3

For information about custom editions, special sales, premium and
corporate purchases, please contact Sterling Special Sales
Department at 800-805-5489 or specialsales@sterlingpublishing.com.

# Table of Contents

# Introduction

**D**o you have a sharp eye? The pairs of pictures in this book may appear to be exactly the same—but they're not! Do you notice anything different? Is something missing? Is there something there that wasn't before? Look closely and see if you can "Spot the Differences."

Puzzles are categorized into three levels of difficulty: Keen, Sharp, and Masterful. There are five differences to "spot" in keen, six in sharp, and seven in masterful. Answers appear at the back of the book.

## Good Luck!

KEEN

Answer on page 126

GARAGE SALE

GARAGE SALE

Answer on page 127

Answer on page 126

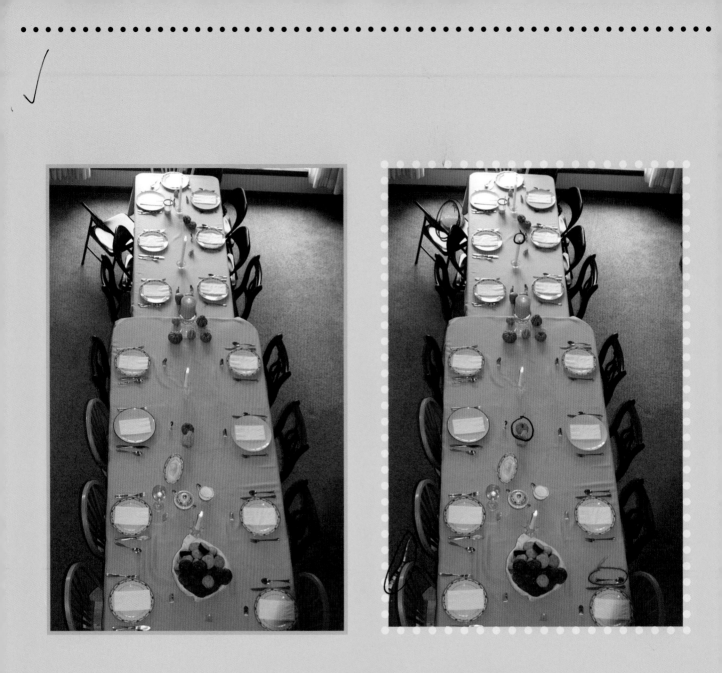

Answer on page 127

Answer on page 128

Answer on page 129

Answer on page 129

Answer on page 130

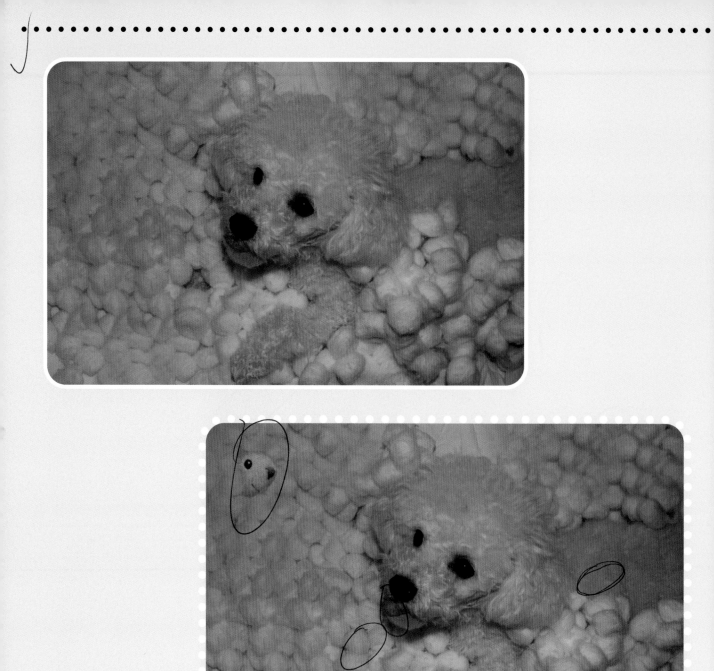

Answer on page 130

Answer on page 131

Answer on page 131

Answer on page 132

Answer on page 132

Answer on page 133

Answer on page 133

Answer on page 134

Answer on page 134

Answer on page 135

Answer on page 135

Answer on page 136

Answer on page 136

Answer on page 137

Answer on page 137

**Answer on page 138**

**Answer on page 138**

Answer on page 139

Answer on page 139

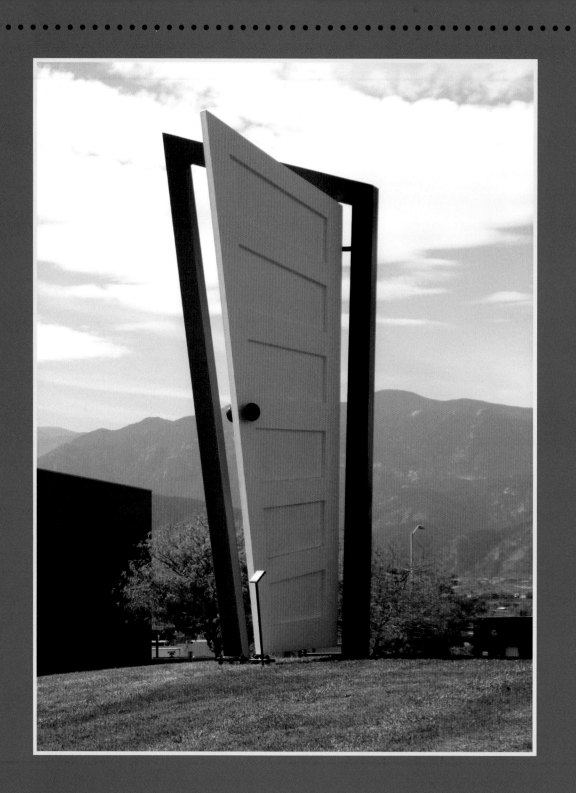

Answer on page 140

Answer on page 140

Answer on page 141

Answer on page 142

Answer on page 141

44

Answer on page 142

**Answer on page 143**

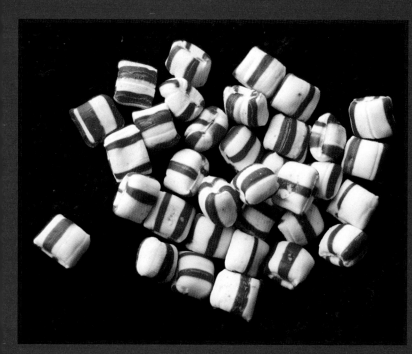

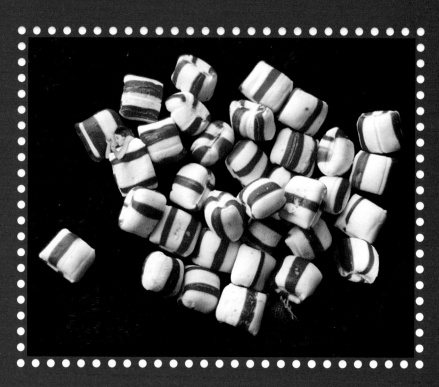

Answer on page 143

Answer on page 144

Answer on page 174

Answer on page 145

Answer on page 145

Answer on page 146

Answer on page 146

Answer on page 147

Answer on page 147

Answer on page 148

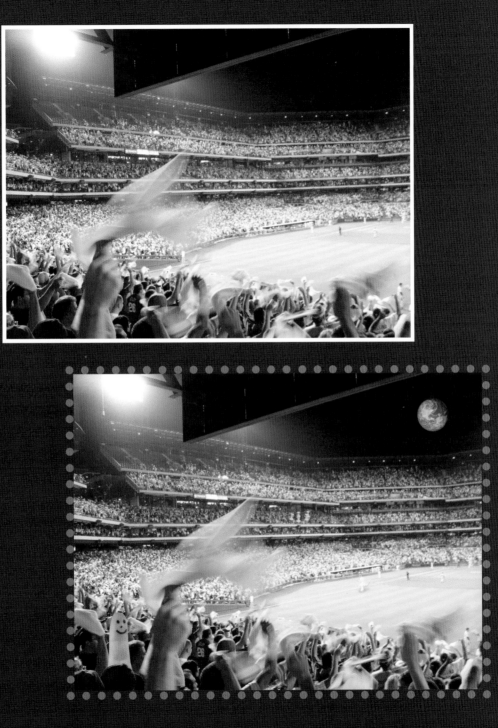

Answer on page 148

Answer on page 149

Answer on page 149

Answer on page 150

Answer on page 150

Answer on page 151

**Answer on page 151**

Answer on page 152

Answer on page 152

**Answer on page 153**

Answer on page 153

Answer on page 154

Answer on page 154

Answer on page 155

**Answer on page 155**

Answer on page 156

Answer on page 156

Answer on page 157

Answer on page 158

Answer on page 158

Answer on page 159

Answer on page 157

# MASTERFUL

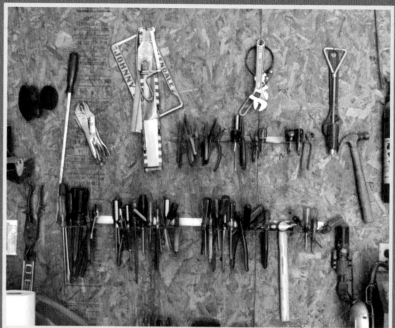

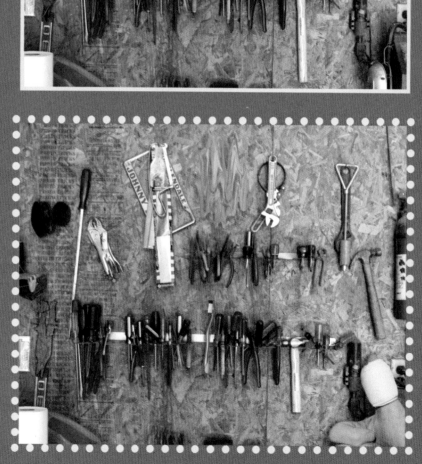

Answer on page 159

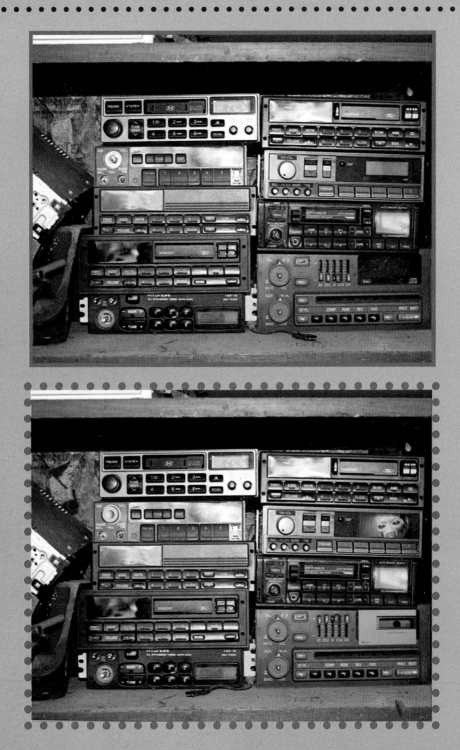

Answer on page 160

Answer on page 160

Answer on page 161

Answer on page 161

Answer on page 162

Answer on page 164

Answer on page 162

Answer on page 163

Answer on page 163

Answer on page 165

Answer on page 164

Answer on page 165

Answer on page 166

Answer on page 166

Answer on page 167

Answer on page 167

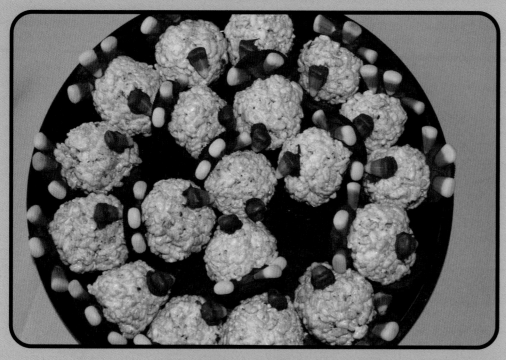

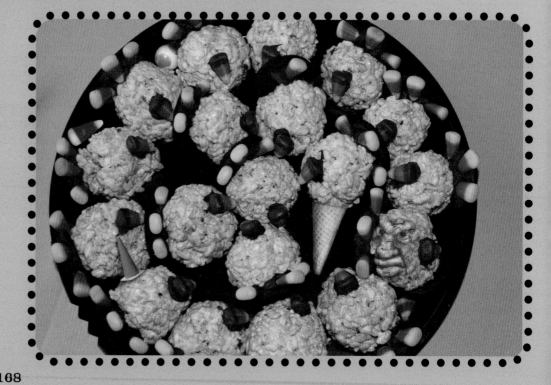

Answer on page 168

Answer on page 168

Answer on page 169

Answer on page 169

Answer on page 170

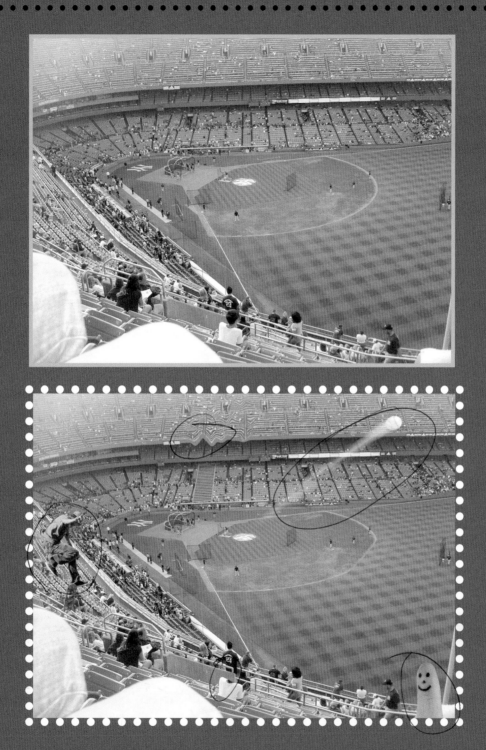

Answer on page 170

Answer on page 171

Answer on page 171

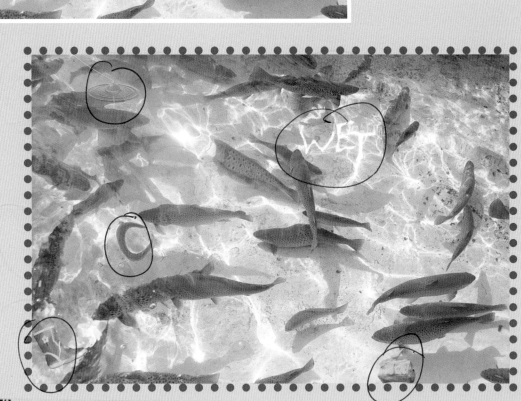

Answer on page 172

Answer on page 172

Kripes! I left the Kennel FOR THIS?!

Answer on page 173

Answer on page 173

Answer on page 174

Answer on page 174

Answer on page 175

Answer on page 175

# ANSWERS

Puzzle page 6

Puzzle pages 8-9

Puzzle page 7

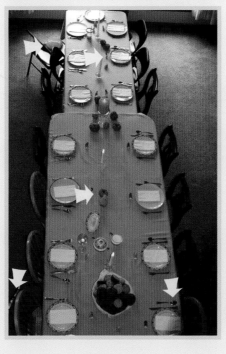

Puzzle page 10

Puzzle page 11

Puzzle page 12

Puzzle page 13

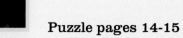

Puzzle pages 14-15

**Puzzle pages 16-17**

**Puzzle page 18**

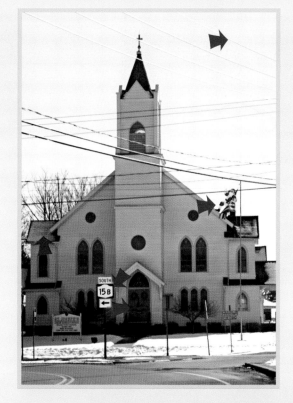

Puzzle page 19

Puzzle page 20

Puzzle page 21

Puzzle page 22

Puzzle page 23

Puzzle page 24

**Puzzle page 25**

**Puzzle page 26**

Puzzle pages 28-29

Puzzle page 27

Puzzle page 30

Puzzle page 31

Puzzle page 32

Puzzle page 33

**Puzzle page 34**

**Puzzle page 35**

Puzzle page 36

Puzzle page 37

**Puzzle pages 38-39**

**Puzzle page 40**

Puzzle page 41

Puzzle page 44

**Puzzle pages 42-43**

**Puzzle page 46**

**Puzzle page 47**

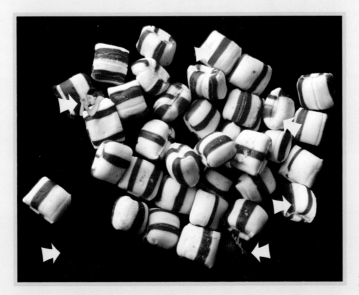

**Puzzle page 48**

**Puzzle page 49**

**Puzzle page 50**

Puzzle page 51

Puzzle pages 52-53

**Puzzle page 54**

**Puzzle page 55**

Puzzle page 56

Puzzle page 57

**Puzzle page 58**

**Puzzle page 59**

Puzzle pages 60-61

Puzzle page 62

**Puzzle page 63**

**Puzzle page 64**

**Puzzle pages 66-67**

**Puzzle page 65**

**Puzzle page 68**

**Puzzle page 69**

Puzzle pages 70-71

Puzzle page 72

Puzzle page 73

Puzzle page 74

Puzzle page 75

Puzzle pages 76-77

**Puzzle page 78**

**Puzzle page 79**

**Puzzle page 86**

**Puzzle pages 80-81**

Puzzle page 82

Puzzle page 83

Puzzle pages 84-85

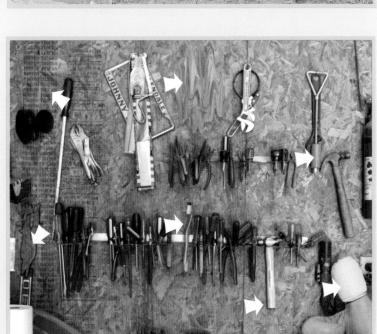

Puzzle page 88

**Puzzle page 89**

**Puzzle page 90**

Puzzle page 91

Puzzle page 92

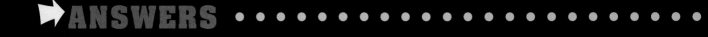

Puzzle page 93

Puzzle page 96

Puzzle page 97

Puzzle page 98

Puzzle pages 94-95

Puzzle pages 100-101

Puzzle page 99

Puzzle page 102

**Puzzle page 103**

**Puzzle page 104**

Puzzle page 106

Puzzle page 105

**Puzzle page 108**

**Puzzle page 109**

Puzzle page 110

Puzzle page 111

Puzzle page 112

Puzzle page 113

**Puzzle page 114**

**Puzzle page 115**

Puzzle page 116

Puzzle page 117

Puzzle page 118

Puzzle page 119

**Puzzle pages 120-121**

**Puzzle page 122**

Puzzle page 123

Puzzle page 124